Adoption is an Option

Your Step-by-Step Guide to Growing Your Family

Regina R. Whitfield Kekessi,
MD, MPH, FACOG

Copyright © 2021 Regina Rae Whitfield Kekessi

All rights reserved. No part of this publication may be reproduced, distributed, or transmitted in any form or by any means, including photocopying, recording, or other electronic or mechanical methods, without the prior written permission of the author, except in the case of brief quotations embodied in critical reviews and certain other noncommercial uses permitted by copyright law. For permission requests, contact the publisher at:

www.Holon.co
ISBN#: 978-1-955342-28-5 (Paperback)
ISBN#: 978-1-955342-29-2 (Hardback)
ISBN#: 978-1-955342-19-3 (eBook)

Published by:

Holon Publishing & Collective Press
A Storytelling Company
www.Holon.co

Contents

Dedication	v
Introduction	ix
Chapter One: The Journey to Adoption	1
Dr. Regina Rae's Story	1
A Mindset Shift Regarding Career	10
A Mindset Shift Regarding Children	11
Reasons to Adopt: Same-Sex Couples	13
Reasons to Adopt: Medical Indication	13
Reasons to Adopt: Providing a Loving Home	14
Expanding Your Village	15
Chapter Two: Your Adoption Type	19
Domestic and International Pros and Cons	20
Closed Adoptions	21
Open Adoptions	21
Private Adoption	23
A Family Member	25
Public Adoption (Foster-to-Adopt)	25
Embryo Adoption	26
Chapter Three: Your Agency	29
Location	29
Services for Birth Mom and Adoptive Couple	30
LGBTQ+ Friendly	32
Religious Affiliation	32
Multilingual	33
Chapter Four: Your Funding	37
Grants	38
Loans	38
Employer	38
Tax Credit	39
Other Options	39
Chapter Five: The Home Study	43
Background Check	44

Training Courses	44
References	44
Assessment Interview	45
Chapter Six: Your Profile Book	**49**
Photo Journal	50
Who You Are	50
Openness	51
Chapter Seven: Finding a Match	**55**
Birth Mom's Profile and Prenatal Care	55
Birth Mom Interview	57
Chapter Eight: Bringing the Baby Home	**63**
Preparing for Your Bundle's Arrival	65
The BIRTH Day	66
Surrender Day	66
Putative Father Registry	67
Chapter Nine: The Final Hurdle	**71**
Establishing a Routine	72
Work-Life Balance	73
Adoption Finalization Day	75
Chapter Ten: Your Life After Adoption	**81**
Changes	83
Nurturing New Relationships	
While Maintaining Old Relationships	84
Updating Important Documents	85
Adjusting Budget	86
Establishing a Village of Support	87
Conclusion	**91**
Our Daughter	92
Resources	**95**

Dedication

To my loving husband and life partner, Etcrhi Kekessi, for your unconditional love, unwavering support, and encouragement to share our amazing journey to parenthood with the world. You are my balance, my voice of reason, and a daily reflection of God's love for me. I love you to the moon and back, and I cannot imagine sharing this life's journey with anyone else.

To my daughter, my heartbeat, who has forever changed my life for the better. Thank you for loving me in a way only a child can love a mother. Thank you for bringing such a bright light to our lives. We look forward to marveling at the woman you will become — the woman God has called you to be.

To my mom, Ollye Lee Bass Whitfield, who has been my rock, my foresight, and who has who has loved me without waiver despite my faults, who has always been there to support my dreams no matter how wild, and who established my mindset early in life that the words "no, never, can't and impossible" were not acceptable in our household. "If it's been done before, it can be done." "Ask for what you want; they can only say yes or no." "The response 'no' often means, 'not right now.'" "Be persistent." "What God has for you is for you."

To my dad, Roy Rogers Whitfield, who left us too soon at the age of 41, for the love and sacrifices you made for your family and our country, and who planted seeds of growth and prosperity we continue to harvest today. I love Daddy, and I always will. Until we meet again.

To my bonus dad Geroy A. Wilkins and to my godfather Robert W. Parker, the two roaring lions who stepped in proudly and without reservation to accept the baton from my father and have not missed a beat in being there as my father figure, and who have continued to show up as if I was their own. I love you both. Thank you for loving me back.

To my brother from another mother, Keven R. Mack, with whom we share the same birthday and our mothers share the same birth month and only a day apart, who has kept things REAL since day 1, who has shared the unconditional love of a sibling, who has witnessed and supported my personal and professional growth from college to current, and who continues to support my life's journey. I love you and am here for you always!

To my Sister Circle, including my bonus mom Portia, those in my wedding party and those with whom our friendship spans more than 40 years who encouraged me, supported me, prayed for me and carried me through when I could not stand. I love each of you without waiver!

To my lifelong mentors and colleagues — J. W. Carmichael, PhD and Sr. Grace Mary Flickinger — both of whom are Professor Emeritus at Xavier University of Louisiana; Air Force Colonel (Ret.) William W. Hurd, MD, MSc, MPH — Professor, Reproductive Endocrinology and Infertility at the University of Birmingham School of Medicine; Julian Solway, MD, Walter L. Palmer Distinguished Service Professor of Medicine and Pediatrics at the University of Chicago Pritzker School of Medicine; and Cynthia E. Boyd, Sr. Vice President, Chief Compliance Officer Rush University System for Health: I am forever grateful to each of you for contributing to who I am today as a physician, educator, researcher, mentor, leader and author in the field of Medicine.

To my pastors Reverend Dr. Richard Nelson of Greater Open Door Baptist Church of Chicago and Pastors Freddie T. & Marsha Piphus of Zion Global Ministries who have and continue to pray for me through some "thangs" and be an ever-present help to support my personal, spiritual and professional journey. May the Lord continue to shine your light for His Glory today and always.

To my business coach and colleague Draion M. Burch, DO, "Dr. Drai," for having the heart, the vision, and the love for the field of medicine to create the Medical Mogul Academy which teaches physicians the business of medicine, helps doctors to recognize their worth beyond the exam room, and provides his formula for financial freedom and generational wealth. You are a godsend Sir. It is a blessing and honor that our lives have crossed paths.

Saint Katharine Drexel and the Sisters of the Blessed Sacrament for making a lifelong commitment to educating African and Native American children and for founding Xavier University of Louisiana — my beloved alma mater.

To my Village of friends, family, church members, sorority sisters, prayer warriors, for being a listening ear and providing words of encouragement along this journey.

To my patients and office colleagues who extended unwavering support to me and my family throughout my journey to parenthood and in the creation of this labor of love.

And last but not least, I dedicate this book to every mother who made the brave, selfless decision to give the gift of life and then extend that gift to countless individuals who have yearned for the gift of parenthood — like us. We are eternally grateful.

In Loving Memory

My Father, Roy Rogers Whitfield (1941-1982)
My Grandfather, Wallace Bass, Sr. (1928-2013)
My Godmother, Bobbie J. Parker (1936-2018)
My Great Grandmother, Connie "Miss Honey" Branch (1910-2000)
My ancestors from the African diaspora on whose shoulders I stand!

Introduction

Are you ready to begin our journey?

When I say "our journey," I am speaking of family planning that can include various causes of infertility and their sequelae. I'm thinking of categories that may render someone unable to have their children without some interventions. So, I could say "our journey," had five contributing factors that led to our infertility journey. They included age, fibroids, no prior pregnancies before the age of 40, abnormal semen analysis, and polycystic ovarian syndrome (PCOS). You can be a single person, and you want to be a parent. You can be a same sex couple who desires to have a family. Perhaps, you can have your own infertility journey. I am writing this book because I want each reader to understand how adoption is an excellent option for growing your family. I'm also a one-of-a-kind doctor with whom you can speak to help with your journey. I believe if we spend a bit of time together, you will soon realize I have walked in your shoes in some capacity or another. I have walked in your shoes while also wearing the medical hat. I have the knowledge and the wisdom of the things that you're going to have to consider for your unique situation. I am a person who is a doctor who is familiar with the journey that has led many to the choice of adoption. I can also provide valuable information about the process to those who have always wanted to adopt. I can give you my personal reflection regarding the pathway to parenthood as well as a medical, professional, and objective perspective on the subject matter.

Wearing my medical hat, I can be a consultant regarding the birth mom's records. I can assess the birth mom's records and tell the adoptive parent, "Hey, these are some things that you might want to ask the doctor about or ask the adoption agency" so as to get all the information needed to make the best informed decision regarding the adoption. Finally, it is important for adoptive parents to know the conditions and scenarios they have the bandwidth to handle, and those they will have a firm stop as he/she/they are considering opportunities for adoption. Understanding the Child Characteristics Checklist for Foster Care and/or Adoption helps to tease out those nuances. Adoption is a conscious, active decision to care for another human being for life. With that said, I believe it is important that adoptive parents have all data possible to make that "eyes wide open" commitment.

There are so many reasons one might choose to adopt. One could have experienced his or her own infertility journey that moved one in the direction to re-evaluate all roads to parenthood. Another may have a medical condition that threatens her very life should she become pregnant including but not limited to a number of heart, kidney and other health concerns. Risky medical conditions like that include the heart condition known as dilated cardiomyopathy and lupus with significant kidney involvement. Same-sex couples may have to consider the complications of a donor egg or sperm donor to grow their family. A single adult wants to be a parent but asks, 'how do I do that without a partner?' The field of reproduction and infertility as well as the roads to parenthood have grown by leaps and bounds in the last 20 years. A broadened enlightenment and acceptance of adoption in open forum discussions have also blossomed in the same time span. This book adds to the body of literature by consolidating pertinent information on the subject matter in one location. You have a journey. Each person reading this book has had a journey. 'What is your journey today? What are you experiencing or what have you experienced?'

I'm writing this book because I want to navigate and coach you through the process of adoption and provide a blueprint to success! I want to be your consultant when you have questions about the birth mom's medical history or you do not understand the conditions outlined on the child characteristics form. I am writing this book because I know people who have made the decision to adopt but are unsure of how to begin the process. I am writing this book for those who are considering adoption but are overwhelmed with the perceived challenges of cost or determining if they've made a sound decision their "match." I want to provide a "one stop shop" location of data that highlights the most important items one considering adoption should understand. I want to highlight the pitfalls of the adoption process I experienced so you don't have to.

Your journey to the "here and now" may not have been an easy one. Nevertheless, I am writing this book to encourage you to NOT GIVE UP on your dream of becoming a parent if that is your heart's desire. YOU CAN BE A PARENT despite the roadblocks you have encountered and the disappointments along the way. If you are reading this book, you have opened your heart and mind to the concept of adoption. I pray this book and its contents makes the process a more seamless one for you. YOU DESERVE IT and MORE!

Are you ready for our journey?! LET'S GO!!

> *Voices of Adoption:*
>
> I always saw myself as a mother whether I was married or not. I just never imagined I would have problems getting pregnant.

Chapter One
The Journey to Adoption

Dr. Regina Rae's Story

I'm Germany-born because my U.S. military father and family were stationed in Heidelberg at the time of my birth.

Army brats move around a lot. If you're a child of a parent in the U.S. Armed Forces, you understand what it means to "get in where you fit in" and learn to adjust.

Being constantly on the move taught me how to be flexible and resilient at a young age. I remember living in Oklahoma, Rhode Island, and Mississippi in the span of four years. Finally, at age nine we settled in Georgia, where I grew up.

I always wanted to become a mom, and like most moms, I never imagined challenges in getting pregnant when ready. Although I was often told growing up that I was the "only one that stuck" after my parents experienced five miscarriages, it still never dawned on me I would meet with similar complications. I would learn the impact fibroids can have on fertility as well as the inheritable nature of the fibroids down the road.

I decided to become a physician at the ripe age of eleven after the untimely death of my father at 41years old. Upon graduating from 8th grade, I transferred from a Fine Arts Magnet program to a Health, Science, and Engineering High School to pursue that dream. I soon recognized the level of responsibility, delayed gratification, and sacrifice the road to medicine required, and I solidified that commitment.

I earned my Bachelor's Degree in Biology, my Master's Degree in Public Health, and worked in the field before beginning medical school at 30 years old. It was during my third year in medical school in the early 2000s, I remember learning about contributors of infertility including how age affected the fertility window, how the quality and number of eggs diminished over time, and what was meant by the "ticking biological clock."

After the birth of the first in vitro fertilization (IVF) baby in 1981, the field of Reproductive Endocrinology took off like wildfire! How lucky was I to be a student doctor amid this technological advancement boom in the industry. My fellow colleagues and I learned about the concepts of egg retrieval, IVF, and then embryo implantation. We learned about intracytoplasmic sperm injection (ICSI) and embryo transfer. Having no partner, I asked, "Can I just freeze one of my embryos?!" The answer was an unfortunate, "no" as only embryos and not eggs were surviving thaw. Fast forward to 2021. Parents now have the choice to freeze and thaw eggs, pair them with the sperm of their choice and then implant. Technology also allows embryos to be tested for genetic abnormalities before being transferred to the uterine cavity for implantation.

Now, you may be asking yourself, why didn't I embrace this advanced embryo technology and set the stage for my future family? To be honest, I did not want the potential ethical dilemma of having a future partner not embrace the embryo because the egg was not fertilized by his sperm. I took my chances and continued my education.

I was blessed beyond measure in 2007 when I met my now husband. It was a whirlwind romance that culminated, and we got married a year and a half later. In 2008, I not only got married, but I also completed my residency, started a new job, moved to a new city, and bought a home with children in mind.

I frequently tell my patients there's never a perfect time to start a family. There's never the perfect amount of money in your bank account. There's never the perfect job. There's never an ideal time where you feel like all of your stars align. You simply reach a place and time and feel comfortable about growing your family.

Although I had thoughts of beginning a family at 38 years old and soon after getting married, it was very important to me that I remained focused to achieve my written and oral boards certification. I did not want to end up like some colleagues who married, had babies, and failed to pass their medical boards because of having to juggle so many responsibilities. That would not be me.

Do you realize individual states have specific medical licensing boards? Some states limit the number of attempts to pass the board exam in your specialty. If you fail to pass your specialty boards within the expected timef rame allowed, one can face the possibility of losing hospital privileges to practice. I have seen others have to move to another state in order to work. That would not be me.

I've known friends who experienced these setbacks, and I saw how it impacted their medical careers. Knowing the facts of a narrowing fertility window as an Obstetrician Gynecologist, it was important to me to secure my professional future so as to care for a future little one. However, to speed up the process, I petitioned the specialty boards for permission to take my written and oral board exams in the same year — 2010.

I knew the risks of taking the oral and written boards together. My stress skyrocketed, but I had to do it and do it successfully in order to move about the business of becoming a mother. Now at 40 years old, I took the oral boards on one Monday, and had surgery to remove fibroids the following Monday. That procedure was called a myomectomy, and a number of fibroids were removed. We now had a uterine factor for infertility corrected for and medicines on board to treat the Polycystic Ovarian Syndrome (PCOS), and were ready to proceed with the next steps.

It's 2011, with my myomectomy surgery behind me, I committed to growing my family via IVF. I want to discuss the complexity of the IVF process, so others can get a true understanding of what the procedure entails.

The process begins with preparing your ovaries for egg retrieval. You often take daily injections to stimulate your ovaries to produce mature cysts. The cyst houses the egg for fertilization. An overstimulation of the ovaries means your ovaries are making a lot of mature cysts — more than the one cyst that is typically generated every month. Once the follicles reach a mature size, the doctor goes in vaginally and, using ultrasound for guidance, sucks those eggs out of the cysts. This is done under mild IV sedation of course.

Picture your ovaries sitting along the sides of your uterus full of mature cysts that have the eggs and fluid in them. The greater the number of mature cysts, the heavier the overall weight of the ovary, and the greater the size of the ovary. All of this can make you feel bloated and uncomfortable. When a woman lies on her back, the ovaries hang towards the back of the uterus. This area between the vagina and the rectum is called the cul de sac. When a Reproductive Endocrinologist (REI) advances a needle through the backside of the cervix or the backside of the vagina, the REI enters the cul de sac, pierce the cyst and sucks the eggs out with an aspirating straw.

You may be asking yourself why I'm sharing such details around the IVF procedure in a story focused on adoption. It's astounding how many women, including me, try IVF not once but several times before considering alternative options to grow their family.

If you are considering IVF and adoption as viable options, I encourage you to visit SART.org, the Society for Artificial Reproductive Technology (SART) website, for additional information, including the success rates of REIs performing IVF procedures. Keep in mind the data may be a year behind as REIs report pregnancy outcomes. Trust me; you'll want to consult SART.org before choosing your IVF Specialist.

I have some other IVF tips to share as someone who's experienced the procedure. Are you comfortable doing self-injections in your butt or hip with a needle? If not, have your partner do it. You'll often need to insert pills into your vagina as well to sustain your uterine lining in preparation for intrauterine placement of the fertilized egg (embryo). There will be frequent doctor's appointments to check the status of the ovaries and the uterine lining and make sure your uterus responds to medicines.

Be ready for uncertainty, feeling bloated, gaining weight, just like being pregnant. Expect multiple ultrasounds to assess the size of the follicular cysts.

After the REI retrieves the eggs through the vagina, they are delivered to the Embryologist who then injects the eggs with a single sperm in the lab and await successful fertilization. The doctor knows when there has been a successful fertilization when the two cells (egg and sperm) begin to divide and grow. When the embryos have reached a certain level of cell division, one or two embryos are placed into the uterine cavity (womb) and the (IVF) process is complete. Then we wait patiently to see if "things took/stuck/implanted."

If you are unable to get healthy eggs, you may have to consider using a donor egg.

Remember what I said about uncertainty? You may have to do this again and again. I should know because not only did I begin my journey at 40, I also had a structural problem with my uterus that could impact my ability to carry a child. Before attempting IVF, I needed to remove fibroids, wait to heal fully, and finally start the IVF process.

Someone undergoing IVF has a number of lab tests drawn prior to the actual process. Some of these labs can include: FSH, LH, TSH, prolactin, Hgb A1c, free and total testosterone, antibody levels against varicella and rubella, Vitamin D and Vitamin B12 levels and the anti-mullerian hormone levels.

Think about everything I just shared with you. Now, try to imagine someone attempting three IVF cycles, two of them with their eggs. That's me, and I still wasn't able to become pregnant. We then decided to try donor eggs. Sadly, I experienced my first miscarriage. Unsurprisingly, we needed to take a break after the heartache.

Since we share a passion for families, you won't be surprised to learn that we started back on the IVF journey when I turned 43. We went back to the same donor, but she had retired from the process. So, we had to consider a different donor. We worked with an out-of-state donor, someone with a good record, paid for her travel to our state, and worked with our physician to yield her eggs.

I began implementing day-to-day medicines and in-person injections to prime my uterus for a fertilized egg (embryo). We were excited about how beautiful the embryos were but saddened by the fact none of the embryos implanted.

It soon became too depressing and difficult to return to the same REI medical practice. Each visit reminded us of what we failed to achieve. So we took our few remaining embryos to a new doctor with different protocols that might deliver success.

Unfortunately, we were met with another disappointment. Our remaining embryos did not survive the thawing process. So we were left with the decision to return to the drawing board. We chose another donor and medical practice with a donor egg program to make another attempt at becoming pregnant. We became pregnant again but miscarried shortly after completing the confirmation ultrasound.

I experienced my final miscarriage at 45 years old. I was at work completing a 24 hour call when I began to bleed. The experience was like deja vu a third time. In between putting a smile as I rounded on and discharged patients, I went to the restroom to change my flooding pad. During the final trip to the restroom, I felt a strong cramp and realized I was passing my baby. I stood up, looked back and retrieved fetal tissues from the toilet. I preserved it in a sterilized cup for further examination to verify the loss and headed back to work. At that very moment as a physician, I had the responsibility of completing my duties. I then removed my doctor's hat, replaced it with a patient hat, and called my own doctor to inform him of the loss.

I became depressed. I started looking at the dollars spent with nothing to show for it but pain and despair. I remember growing angry and resentful over money that I could have applied towards student loans. You've probably examined the costs as well if you've been in my shoes.

It became very difficult to go to work on a daily basis and be happy for a patient who had achieved the success that so far eluded me. It became difficult to manage patients who exercised their right to end their pregnancy, while I struggled to realize one for myself. I still remember a patient coming in, African-American, and pregnant with twins. She said, "you know what? I already have three. I'm not trying to have any more." I asked her, "have you considered adoption?" Her response was, "if I have to carry them to term, I might as well keep them, and I'm not doing that!" I stood there wearing my medical hat speechless thinking, "I'll take your babies" but I could not say that out loud! Ohhh, how I had yearned for twins to break the family's "only child syndrome." Unfortunately, the patient elected to abort.

I have already told you that I am an only child. What I didn't tell you was that I am the only child of an only child (my Mom) of an only child (my grandmother). I was the only child of my parents. How was I going to carry on the Whitfield name? I considered asking a young cousin to donate her eggs for the cause until I had a horrific nightmare that showcased an awkward moment at a family reunion in which my child's true identity was revealed by an uncle in a drunken stupor!!

We made a final appointment to prepare for another frozen embryo transfer. I was so emotionally spent, I forgot to show up for an important ultrasound appointment to determine whether my uterine lining was ready for another frozen embryo transfer (FET). As a doctor who never misses a medical appointment, I realized the harsh reality of our need to stop and re-evaluate our options. It was at this time, we really had to ask ourselves what we really wanted to achieve. Was it more important for me to feel a child growing inside of me or to experience the joy of having a child to mold and raise as our own? After deep reflection, we realized it was the latter.

After exhausting all the fertility options over five years, including two IVF cycles with my own eggs, a fresh IVF cycle with three egg donors and numerous FETs, and three miscarriages, medical considerations began to shift toward my husband's sperm as a potential contributor to our infertility. It was at that very moment I told my husband, who's seven years older than me, "If we have to consider a donor egg and now a donor sperm, that sounds like an adoption to me. Let's save ourselves from any further headache, aggravation, and frustration and consider adoption!" It was at that very moment, the fog of depression began to lift and the remote chance of becoming parents became a possibility again.

I know I shared a lot of details, and honestly, a lot of heartache. I want to show the whole journey and process that led me to where I am today.

With a firm decision in place to proceed with adoption, I decided to focus more on my health so I could be in the best shape possible to enjoy my child when he/she arrived. I met with a Cardiologist to address my concerns of heart disease since my father died from a massive heart attack at 41 years old. To prolong my life, Dr. H. recommended that I work on losing weight, eating better, and decreasing the stress in my life."

We decided to make ourselves and our health the top priorities.

During the next two years, my husband and I decided to make ourselves and our health the top priorities. We both lost weight, incorporated better eating habits and focused on the adoption process. We connected with our first adoption agency and were matched with a young lady who was having a boy. Unfortunately, the match fell through and we were met with another disappointment. However, we pushed through the pain and remained focused. We connected with a 2nd adoption agency, we were matched with a young lady who was firm in her decision, and we were on track to welcome our daughter into the world. Then a BOMBSHELL!

Two weeks before our daughter arrived, I received the diagnosis of breast cancer.

Yep. Your eyes are not deceiving you; You read that right. BREAST CANCER! After all that we had been through to get to this point in our lives?! What in the world was happening? Was my cancer related to my fertility treatments? Although research does not support this medical hypothesis, I could not help thinking about how cancer had shown its ugly head. No one else in my family had suffered from breast cancer, so I thought. After some research, I identified breast, pancreatic and colon cancer on my maternal grandfather's side.

Although none of this made sense, I looked to my faith and asked the Lord for clarity. If things could not get worse, I was informed the Friday before my daughter's arrival that my employer's benefit plan did not cover maternity leave for adoptive parents. Really???? So I am expected to go on leave for six weeks to bond with my child without pay?? How was that okay?

Well my God answered ALL of those questions and more. Although I had no maternity benefits, the diagnosis of breast cancer gave me full benefits. This allowed me to receive appropriate management for the new diagnosis and spend a full three months at home bonding with our precious arrival. So you see. "We know that all things work together for good to them that love God, to them who are the called according to his purpose" (Romans 8:28

KJV), and the Lord had things orchestrated for my good all along.

Our daughter arrived safely on a Sunday evening, we brought her home safely that Friday. The following Wednesday, I underwent a seeding procedure to locate the area of resection, and the following day underwent a lumpectomy. I underwent a wider resection of the following to assure clear margins. While some see that as a setback, we saw it as a victory because additional cancer cells were identified!

Know that in order to have a testimony, you must go through a test. Otherwise, all you will have are the "monies,"...moaning about this and moaning about that.

A Mindset Shift Regarding Career

Even as an experienced doctor, I still question what medical school truly prepares you to do. You may think about this, too. I'm convinced that medical school prepares one to see patients. The role of the physician is to manage patients and provide clinical care.

It is our mission. It is part of our Hippocratic oath to do no harm. Having gone through what I've been through, my experience highlights the need for a plan B, C, and D to ensure that lifes' goals are met.

Nobody talks about private practice models in medical school because malpractice insurance is too high. It's also challenging to balance your role as a clinician seeing patients and as an operations manager growing a business. Unless you're laser-focused on establishing a private practice, it likely won't happen.

Working in medicine is all about team building, teamwork, and taking one for the team. Faculty promote cooperation in med school, but medicine is also a competitive business. You think about every action and choice that impacts your bottom line.

By this point in the book, you have a good sense of who I am and what motivates me. I love my career but a healthy work life balance is paramount. I believe in working hard and playing harder. I'm a transplant in Ohio who completed my residency elsewhere. I didn't know anybody, and I worked hard at changing that.

I made it a personal mission to meet primary care docs in the city. I made lists containing the names of OB-GYN, pediatricians, family practice physicians, and internal medicine docs. I wrote personal letters. I reached into my pocket and sent home baked cookies and desk calendars. I wanted to be considered a good partner in the city's medical community. I also wanted to be a good salesperson and convince providers to refer patients to me. I invested in my practice in order to build my practice.

The life I've lived thus far, and the COVID pandemic has given room for pause, and has moved me to become more intentional with my work and my decision making. I'm still learning how to appreciate the fruits of my labor while enjoying what I do. However, there has to be a way to generate income and not compromise my original reasons for going into medicine. I am finding my way.

A Shift in Mindset Regarding Children

Three generations of key women comprise my family story. My mom raised me as an only child which means that I am accustomed to being self-sufficient. She called me her miracle baby because she had five miscarriages due to fibroids, and I was the only pregnancy that stuck. There's my grandmother; and a great-grandmother with seven siblings! My dad's family is more extensive, with lots of uncles and aunts.

When I reflect on the intimacy of my mother's family, I think that's why I wanted more than one child. You know that it did not turn out that way for me, and in hindsight, I don't know if I can handle more than one child. I applaud colleagues and friends raising as many as four children, including twins!

I suppose that some parents make a beeline towards adoption. You learned from my story to date that our path contains zigs and zags.

I won't lie that I felt relief over taking a break from all the medications. I smiled upon learning that adoption can be cheaper than another IVF cycle.

My research involved talking to patients who were adopted. They eagerly shared their experiences, and I enjoyed listening to their stories.

Learning from my adopted patients helped keep me from becoming discouraged. I admit that I prayed a lot, saying, "God, if this is not your will for me to have a child, then tell me that and take this desire from me so I can concentrate on something else." The yearning remained.

OB-GYNs know more than many people how much we crave control, especially around pregnancies. We want to know a specific delivery date. Parents want to learn the baby's gender. My journey towards becoming a parent reveals the value of taking each day as it comes. I now tell patients that our babies are really in control of their pregnancies, and we manage our pregnancies by what the babies show us. It's a fluid process. You can't control others, but you can help yourself by staying healthy, taking prenatal vitamins, and staying fit. That's what you can control.

For me, being fluid and understanding what I can and can't control leads to my decision on adoption. It also helps clarify what's important to my husband and me.

We want a child. Is it unacceptable unless I can feel it in my belly? No. Does the child have to come from my genetics? No. We want a child that we can impact, influence, and who can influence our lives as well. That's what's important to us, and I imagine it's important to you.

Reasons to Adopt: Same-Sex Couples

I want to focus for the moment on same-sex couples looking to adopt and the importance of identifying agencies that are welcoming.

I live in Ohio, a conservative state, and I've witnessed adoption agency staff passing judgment on same-sex couples. It's not right, nor fair, but it is a reality. However, a child waiting for a parent to love them is the one who pays the price of unfairness. Yet, it is great to know that even through the unfairness, same-sex couples are given a chance to love the children who so need love. I encourage you to pay attention to adoption agency websites, social media posts, ads, and brochures. You'll learn how accepting they are of same-sex couples. Choose a supportive agency who will help you meet your goal.

Same-sex female couples also have additional work if considering fertility treatments. They have to think about which mom will carry the baby. Same-sex couples have to consider the medical conditions of each pelvis and a potential carrier's health. A decision is often decided on who will make the ideal mom for carrying and giving birth to the baby. They also have to determine their source for sperm. Is it a mutual friend that they trust? Is it a family member like a brother? Is it less complicated to use a sperm bank? Nobody wants a legal battle down the road with the sperm donor claiming parental rights.

With regard to same sex male couples, a decision is often made to either go with an egg donor or work with a surrogate who also provides the egg. There's also a decision as to who will be the father of the child or children. It's not fair, but there's extra work for same-sex parents.

Reasons to Adopt: Medical Indication

Sadly, some medical conditions lead doctors to recommend against pregnancy because of life risks. A woman who experienced a kidney transplant is an example of a risky medical condition. Kidney transplants lie in the front part of the lower abdomen, and a growing uterus may prevent it from functioning at an appropriate capacity. A woman who becomes pregnant in the setting of dilated cardiomyopathy is at a greater than 50% chance of death should she carry the pregnancy to term. There are a number of chronic conditions that can worsen during the pregnancy process that may not be in the best interest of the patient.

If you're someone choosing adoption due to a medical condition, take comfort in the fact that you're not alone.

Reasons to Adopt: Providing a Loving Home

Preparing a loving home for your child leads to important questions about becoming good parents. What are your driving desires to become parents?

For me, a loving home involves: Sharing wisdom with your child; Molding them, and providing a chance for a better outcome.

This goal does not change between a birth child and an adoptive child. The positive impact on the parent also remains the same. You learn how to be less selfish, give more and extend new opportunities to someone else.

While writing this section, my mind fell on a colleague who had seven children, one of whom is adopted. I contemplate the importance of sacrifice in parenting. Having a child means that you are no longer the number one priority. You no longer focus on living the life you always wanted. You're in the backseat, and your child occupies the front seat.

I know some people stumble into parenthood via an unplanned pregnancy and they do just fine. Adoption, on the other hand, requires planning, and planning makes one think about parenting roles and responsibilities. You become a parent with your eyes wide open about the possibilities and responsibilities of caring for a child.

Remember, I'm a later-in-life doctor, and I'm a later-in-life parent. Our parents are older, and we may not always have the advice and support of our parents. That's okay. We can still be successful and find help elsewhere.

Like many professional career women, my education took priority over dating and relationships. I remember hearing time and time again that "the boys can wait, they were here before you were born and they will still be here when you die". Consider a girlfriend of mine, who was 40 at the time (with no partner and a desire to have a baby. She had the resources to pursue IVF treatments and became pregnant with twins. Although she did not have a partner to help with parenting, she had her mother and extended family.

Expanding Your Village

Later-in-life parents like my husband and I can appreciate help just like the next couple. Unfortunately, the reality is our parents are older and we cannot reasonably rely on them indefinitely due to their age. My mom helps with our daughter, but she's 75 and moving slower. She's past the time of getting on the floor and playing with a grandchild.

My mom participates as much as possible, and my husband and I expect nothing more from her. We would never ask for more from our parents. However, we do seek out other friends to join our village of support.

Do you know what I like about seeking support from family and friends? It forces you to let your guard down, become vulnerable, and catalog your shortcomings as a parent.

Expanding your support village leads you to the truth that you cannot do everything. In the 24/7 whirlwind of raising a child, you, my blessed parent, will often need help. I don't care if you're a stay-at-home mom or stay-at-home dad. Every parent, no matter the workload, needs help sometimes. Every parent will eventually trust the care of their child with a babysitter, caregiver, or family friend.

You may fight the urge. I know I did. I didn't want anybody in my house near my baby. My husband stayed home for the first year, so we wouldn't need to send our daughter to daycare. We tried to do it all, and I would be lying if I didn't admit to being exhausted from refusing to open my home to people willing to help.

When you expand your support village, you simultaneously lower your guard dog instincts and identify people to trust with your child. Inviting people to join your village does not require compromising on safety. You'll always choose caregivers carefully. You'll probably become a nanny expert capable of identifying a solid support person at a glance.

I started trusting my instincts, which led me to befriend one of the environmental service workers. I could tell by her early morning dedication and energy that she was special. We also shared the hospital prayer room on many occasions. I consider her a friend as well as a trusted member of my support tribe.

There are many reasons why people chose to adopt. However, there is a common thread among them all — a desire to raise a child in a loving and giving home.

Notes

Voices of Adoption:

I couldn't see any of the men I was dating being worthy of being my child's father.

Chapter Two
Your Adoption Type

There are universal themes, whether expanding your family with a new baby or adoption. Adoption may come with hefty expenses, but adoptive and biological parents share much in common after the high costs.

Think about time. When your child, whether adoptive or biological, is due to arrive, you must have the available time to care for and raise it. You need sufficient funds. You also need an established support system, or what I refer to as a 'support village.'

Some babies are unplanned. The intentional nature of adoption forces parents to plan for a new child. It's a good thing.

Practice careful financial planning when considering the costs of daycare and school. Do you have your village of supporters who can help when you and your spouse are at work? There will be a time when your child has a fever, will need to come home from school, but you won't be available.

A strong supportive network won't stop all unexpected problems, but it will provide you with people who can help you take care of them.

Establishing your adoption type requires adoptive parents to identify what's important even before things begin.

Do you consider adoption agency fees as a top priority? It is important you find something in your budget.

Ask yourself if the adoption agency advocates your needs as well as the needs of your partner? Do they have separate staff supporting the adoptive parents and birth mother or the same team?

Answers to your growing list of questions arrive when you start to understand adoption categories.

A recent conversation with a patient helps clarify how different types of adoption resonate with other parents.

One of my IVF patients ends a pregnancy after learning of a life-threatening malformation. There are few decisions harder than ending a baby's life because you know it won't survive. The heartbreaking experience makes her hesitant about pursuing an IVF cycle for a second time. She desperately wants to raise a girl and wonders what types of adoption can help her.

Listening to my patient talk about her needs reminds me of the importance of choosing the right agency and type of adoption for your goals and needs. There are lots of factors, big and small, to consider. Let's get started.

Domestic and International Pros and Cons

The name Domestic Adoption captures what you need to know. Prospective parents are adopting a child in the 50 states in the United States. International Adoption means the child will be coming from outside the US. Domestic Adoption contains fewer law requirements. International Adoption takes longer due to the US and hosts country law requirements.

Fewer law requirements increase a parent's chances for receiving their baby soon after birth in Domestic Adoption. International Adoption parents frequently receive their babies six months after delivery or later due to governmental red tape and delays.

International Adoption delays wipe away opportunities to bond with your baby during its earliest months. International Adoption adds opportunities to learn new cultures, including new languages. Bringing home a baby via International Adoption makes your home multicultural. It's a beautiful gift. Your International baby may come from an impoverished nation. Your decision may result in chances for a better life. It's an extra value that makes the red tape and delays feel manageable.

Closed Adoptions

When a birth mom gives up her child with no interest regarding the parents' identity, that's a Closed Adoption.

In a Closed Adoption, the birth mom never receives any information about the adoptive parents. The birth mom's concern is securing an agency to take her baby at delivery and safely hand her baby to the best adoptive parents.

The process behind a Closed Adoption is amazingly lean. The agency writes a summary of the birth mom's medical and social histories. They record health information from her OB-GYN visit and physical to share with adoptive parents. That's it, nothing more. The birth mom passes on the opportunities to choose her baby's parents. The communication and information between birth mom and adoptive parents are mostly "closed" and remain closed for years depending on each state.

Open Adoptions

Open Adoptions contain multiple contacts between the birth mom and the adoptive parents. The degree of communication and openness vary by case. Maybe the birth mom wants to retain some form of contact with her baby after the adoption. The birth mom and adoptive parents may agree to emails and photos. They'll decide on the number of messages and the timing. There may even be onsite visits at a restaurant or playground.

Open Adoptions offer birth moms and adoptive parents various messaging options. Agencies always promote good-faith agreements between the parties. Agencies want the birth mom to exit the process feeling confident about the future welfare of her baby. Adoptive parents want the chance to build a new and independent family. Perhaps Open Adoptions can also be described as win-win adoptions.

Adoptions continue to change over time, and Open Adoptions reflect these changes. The era of behind-closed-door transactions between a birth mom and the adoptive parents is over.

Open discussions about adoption are the norm, and adoption leaders believe adoptive children transition better with increased transparency from adoptive parents. The more information adoptive children receive from parents, the less they question the love of their adopted family.

You may know someone adopted who didn't look anything like their parents and wanted to learn as much info as possible about their extended family. You probably have an adopted friend or co-worker content to know very little about their birth mom.

My husband and I followed agency advice and created a unique email address for our adopted daughter. That way, if our daughter's birth mom wants to reach her, or if our daughter has questions for her, they have a unique line of communication.

Our communication plan for our daughter involved quarterly emails and pictures with an agreement to re-evaluate the situation on her first birthday.

It's worth noting that the birth mom's emails stopped when our daughter turned one. We have the birth mom's contact email and medical records to help reconnect if our daughter wants to learn more when she's older.

Our version of an Open Adoption includes quarterly emails during our daughter's first year. I know other parents who meet the birth mother quarterly and maintain a relationship. They treat the birth mom as a co-parent in an extended family. The birth mom may have other children, so your child has the chance to connect with birth siblings.

Other adoptive parents learn of a birth mom's addiction or abusive past. They decide that communication with the birth mom comes at high risk for harming the child. For them, it's best to shut down communication.

Maybe the birth mom lives nearby, and you want to avoid too-frequent visits and the chance of her investigating your family on social media.

I think about this as a rare African-American OB-GYN in Greater Cincinnati who used a Cincinnati adoption agency to connect with our first birth mom. The birth mom moved from the decision of a closed adoption to an open one with quarterly visits. We were not interested in co-parenting, and the close proximity would have been less than ideal.

There's no one right way to adopt. Open adoption occurs on a spectrum, and the levels of openness vary widely. I think it depends on what the participants want and see. I know what I want, and it's for my adoptive daughter to be clear about who her parents are.

Private Adoption

Prospective parents interested in adoption have choices other than working with the Administration for Children and Families and public adoption agencies. They also have opportunities to work with private adoption agencies and attorneys functioning as intermediaries between the birth mom and adoptive parents.

Private Adoption agencies come at a higher cost due to legal fees from adoption attorneys, home studies, medical care for the birth mom, social work services, stipends for the birth mom, and post-placement assistance.

Chances are you've used an attorney by now for a family will or a car accident. Do you realize there are adoption attorneys who only work on adoptions? I have a tip for finding the right adoption attorney for you.

The Academy of Adoption and Assisted Reproduction Attorneys lists approximately 470 attorneys experienced in adoption laws and regulations.

Adoptive parents are responsible for private adoption costs, including attorney fees. There's some room for negotiation. State governments forbid direct gifts to a birth mom to prevent the impression of parents "buying" a baby.

Adoptive parents frequently donate baby supplies to an agency that distributes the supplies to the birth mom and others. While this method of donating baby supplies may appear complex, the goal is crystal clear. You want to help the birth mom and new baby be as healthy as possible.

The costs add up in Private Adoption, but the birth mom and baby's care remain a top priority. You may not realize this advance, but the inherent privacy of a Private Adoption helps everyone involved.

Maybe the birth mom is a teenager facing an unwanted pregnancy? Perhaps you and your partner want to keep your family planning decisions private?

When you consider the shorter wait for your baby, the more personalized service, the support of an attorney in charge of the legal paperwork, and high-quality health services for the birth mom and baby, Private Adoption may be worth every penny.

A Family Member

When you adopt a family member, there are often unique circumstances involving loss of capabilities or life. You may think that the need for adoption agencies and attorneys fade because you're dealing with known family members.

The truth is taking on financial responsibility for the adopted child requires legal representation and paperwork. An adoption attorney and agency help establish boundaries and represent your positions.

There's always the risk of the birth mom or dad believing they're newly capable of raising their child and wanting the child back.

An adoption attorney will establish guidelines that prevent that scenario from happening and protect your goals for providing the child with opportunities for a happy and healthy life.

Public Adoption (Foster-to-Adopt)

Public adoption agencies arrange meetings between prospective adoptive parents, social workers, family services supervisors to match foster children with forever families. Sometimes, agencies use placement committees to make decisions. The goal of reconnecting a foster child with their birth mom and biological family remains constant. When a home situation puts the child at risk, public adoption agencies initiate legal proceedings to terminate birth parents' legal rights and place the child in an adoptive family. The chance for communication between the birth mom and adopted parents is slim. Public adoption agencies see a separation between the foster child and biological family as healthy and safe.

The large number of children in the foster system waiting for new families is well known. They are a wide variety of ages. Many foster children possess special needs, and some have siblings hoping to stay together.

There are additional steps regarding education and preparation for adoptive parents of foster children. The extra work can be fulfilling, especially for adoptive parents willing to bring an older child to their family.

Embryo Adoption

Here's an adoption fact you may not know. There are over a million embryos in long-term storage in the United States, thanks to people who do not want to discard their unused embryos. I'm not going to start the discussion regarding if an embryo is a baby before eight weeks of development. That's a topic for a different book. What I want to touch upon is the opportunities around embryo adoption.

The technology is evolving, and more states are approving the adoption process as demand from adoptive parents grows.

Embryo adoption provides alternate choices from egg and sperm donors and high-cost IVF cycles. Viability is not a given with embryo adoption. When an embryo grows to maturity, the adoptive mom can carry her baby to term. That fact alone may attract adoptive parents to this future tech option.

The legal process for Embryo Adoption is as unique as the tech behind the storage. An embryo donor lawyer implements securing an IVF facility for managing medical treatment and transferring rights from the embryo donors to the embryo recipients. Most often, embryo recipients travel to the facility storing the embryos. They don't want the risk of shipping.

Are you interested in joining the growing community of Embryo Adoption families? Maybe you're thinking about becoming an embryo donor? Learn more at the National Embryo Donation Center and the National Registry for Adoption.

Notes

> *Voices of Adoption:*
>
> **Sometimes you're so eager to get a child, you don't want to rock the boat. But it's important to carefully evaluate the adoption agency you work with.**

Chapter Three
Your Agency

What do you think you need in an adoption agency? It's the next best question after determining the type of adoption that exceeds your goals and needs. Do you know what's important to me? I value availability. I want an agency with an 800 phone number, a director who's always available, and an open-door policy to hear my concerns.

Other agency characteristics play essential roles. How many successful matches have they made? Are they up to speed with technology? What's the size of their support staff? A small adoption agency grants adoptive parents plenty of autonomy. They're perfect for the do-it-yourself types. If you require handholding and plenty of support, you'll want an agency with a larger team.

Choosing Your Agency, the one that answers your questions, exceeds your needs, and solves your problems, prevents disappointments further down the road. Choosing Your Agency, the one that fits you best reduces the chance of regretting your decision to become an adoptive parent. Regret is the one thing you never want to experience as a parent.

Location

You may not be thinking about agency location, but it's essential.

Here's an example. You're adopting a LatinX child. Seek out an adoption agency located in a community with a large Latino population. If you live in a state with a small Latino population, say, West Virginia, you may seek out agencies in states with sizable Latino communities like California and Texas.

There's another factor involving agency location that may surprise you. Adoption processes vary by state. Your location choice impacts the length of time for the adoption. The average adoption process in Texas runs three months. In Ohio, where my family and I live, the process takes at least six months. Location matters.

Services for Birth Mom and Adoptive Couple

I remember the first adoption agency we visited. It was rather small. The agency director functioned as the support staff for the birth mom and the adoptive parents. I needed equal support between the birth and adoptive moms, but the agency owners leaned towards the birth mom. The agency owners told me that I needed to adjust to the birth mom's needs because she was carrying the baby.

The birth mom would cancel and reschedule appointments at the last minute, and I was expected to manage my patients and office responsibilities in the same manner if I had planned to support her appointments. When I expressed that would not be feasible and frankly, irresponsible to my patients, I was told, "when that baby comes, the world stops!" I remember saying to the agency, "You, as an agency, need to help her to understand the level of responsibility that is shared. I have to work to pay you for this transaction. I'm not going to cancel a full day of patients simply because the patient wanted to sleep in late.

Suddenly, the challenge of sole agency staffers to support birth moms and adoptive moms became clear. I believe the agency felt that I placed my career over the adoption when I complained about canceled appointments. If the agency provided separate team members for birth and adoptive moms, these conflicts would be addressed and solved.

The agency confirmed my assumptions when the Director told me, "The birth mom is our number one priority." I felt disposable listening to the agency boss. I felt like the agency was telling me, "Well, if you don't get on well with the birth mom, we'll find another couple. But we can't always find another baby."

This experience taught me the importance of selecting agencies with sufficient staff to support both the birth mom and the adoptive parents independently.

Please learn from my experiences. Ask the agency if they have a dedicated team member taking the birth mom to her medical appointments. Look at agency websites to learn how they break down services or employ a staff member to handle all medical communications. Do they have a nurse on their team? Taking these extra steps will prevent situations like what I experienced. Even if you're not a medical doctor, like me, you'll have many healthcare-related questions about the birth mom.

Consider all possible situations that require medical transparency. Does the birth mom have a history of alcohol or drug abuse and if so what's the impact on the baby? Will my baby suffer from fetal alcohol syndrome or withdrawal symptoms? Who's providing the medical information? Do I need to secure an impartial OB-GYN? You'll need clear answers before signing on the dotted line of the adoption agreement.

You'll want to ask questions about birth mom and adoptive mom medical history choosing your agency. If you're a first-time adoptive couple without a pediatrician, these questions are critical. You'll need honest medical guidance, whether from the agency or someone you bring to the adoption process. You'll want an accurate review of the birth mom's medical history to make confident decisions about your future family. Ask, no, demand the agency to have the birth mom sign a release to her medical records. You've been open about your medical history. It's only fair that the birth mom is equally transparent. Review the records with adoption agency leadership and save them to share later with your adopted child.

Adoptive parents are understandably nervous and don't want to rock the boat regarding the birth mom's feelings and relations with the adoption agency. Think of fighting for the birth mom's medical records as the first of many battles supporting your child.

The last thing you want to do is question your decision to adopt and turn back.

LGBTQ+ Friendly

There's good news for same-sex couples that want their adoption agencies to be judgment-free. LGBTQ-friendly adoption agencies are standard, and there are available directories. Too many same-sex couples have experienced discriminatory treatment, especially from faith-based adoption agencies. Adoption is emotionally demanding. It's important for adoptive parents, especially same-sex parents, to feel comfortable throughout the adoption process. The good news is that trends continue to support same-sex parents. Bethany Christian Services, the largest Christian adoption agency in the United States, has begun working with LGBTQ+ parents. For same-sex couples hoping for adoption services free of bias, the landscape looks brighter.

Religious Affiliation

Talking about tolerance for LGBTQ+ adoptive parents raises an important change underway in the adoption and child welfare services industry. The time where nearly all adoption agencies partnered with religious organizations is coming to a close. A growing diverse community of adoptive parents can select from a more diverse network of adoption agencies. It's a sign of increased tolerance that benefits everyone in the world of adoption.

Multilingual

Bilingual adoptive parents want to work with agency team members who can communicate in their first language, whether Spanish, French, or whatever. It's an early commitment towards establishing a multilingual home for their adopted child. Some languages, say, Swahili, may be difficult to find agency support. It's important to know that many hospitals have interpreters on-site and are available by phone. If you need someone to answer your adoption questions in Swahili, you'll be able to get somebody on the line.

Notes

Notes

Voices of Adoption:

Ask your employer and/or your partner's employer about adoption benefits. They do not always advertise this service.

Chapter Four
Your Funding

I'm not wealthy — can I still adopt?

Adoption costs vary widely based on choosing a private or foster adoption agency. States have different fees, and allowances regarding the amount of financial support adoptive parents may provide a birth mom.

Are you looking for an adoption fee benchmark? My husband and I paid roughly $23,000 for our adoption, minus some grants and loans. I highly recommend that you budget and itemize your adoption like any significant project. You'll want to account for every dollar spent.

Don't let sticker shock dissuade you from adoption. Some foundations provide financial assistance to adoptive parents. Some support comes directly from the adoption agencies. Through my adoption agency, my husband and I received a grant for blankets and other baby items. Other agencies have access to grants helping adoptive parents offset the costs of adoption or IVF treatments.

There's no reason for any adoptive parent to accept the entire cost of adoption. Research as simple as a Google search will lead to adoption agencies, employers, and foundations that provide funds and grants to adoptive parents. Isn't it great learning that there are people and places that want to help you grow your family?

Grants

Qualification criteria vary for adoption grants coming from governmental and private organizations. Your income will likely determine your eligibility for funds. Some organizations have a ceiling for the number of grant awardees. My general rule of thumb is that pennies add up to dollars, meaning any grant, no matter how small the dollar amount, helps. Investigate. Learn what's out there to help adoptive parents. Embrace the financial support.

Loans

Would you borrow money to cover adoption fees? Of course, you'd use credit cards, bank loans, and private loans to grow your family. To pay our remaining adoption fees, my husband and I withdrew money from our retirement savings. There are plenty of rules around borrowing money from a retirement account like a 401(k). You'll likely want to talk to a financial advisor.

Our financial tech era means adoptive parents have plenty of choices, from traditional banks to online lenders like LendingTree, SoFi, and Best Egg. If you're looking for $100 or $10,000 to zero out your adoption fees, do whatever it takes to grow your family.

Employer

The number of companies providing adoption assistance continues to grow. Ask your employer if they offer adoption benefits. The answers may surprise you.

I know companies that cover costs associated with a single IVF treatment per year. The tip is to speak to HR department staff or insurance representatives to identify all adoption-related funds.

My employer-sponsored health insurance has an annual $5000 cap on fertility-related expenses, whether medicines, injections, or ultrasounds. I'm responsible for adoption costs over $5,000 where I work, but the coverage makes a big difference.

While talking to HR staff about adoption benefits, confirm your employer's maternity and parental leave policies for adoptive parents. Like adoption-related funds, the benefits vary from company to company.

If your employer's leave policy for adoptive parents is minimal to non-existent, I know my hospital's policy comes up short, pursue the Family and Medical Leave Act. The idea is to leave to seek every option for adoption support.

Tax Credit

Nonrefundable tax credits are available up to $14,300 for qualified adoption expenses involving eligible children. The goal for the tax credits is to make adoption affordable for more families. There are numerous rules and frequently asked questions regarding adoption tax credits. Be sure to speak to a financial advisor to gain all the available tax benefits.

Other Options

If you have a strong network of supporters, you have other options to help make adoption a reality. Would you feel comfortable asking a family member, say a sibling, or parent, for a loan? Are there close friends willing to help offset your adoption costs? It's surprising to discover the number of unexpected assets you have to source for funds. Maybe you have a life insurance policy your parents purchased a long time ago that holds cash value you can access.

Are you familiar with crowdfunding platforms like Indiegogo, Kickstarter, and GoFundMe? Crowdfunding allows people to share a project: If the project is to adopt a baby; then people are willing to invest as little as $10 to help you make it happen.

Remember me talking about a "support village." Well, crowdfunding provides opportunities to scale your "support village" with people you've never met. My core advice regarding crowdfunding is to pay attention to the funding window. Crowdfunding can help launch a project. It's not an ongoing source of resources. After using crowdfunding to pay the initial adoption fees, you'll be responsible for raising your adopted child.

Notes

Voices of Adoption:

Pick references based on people who know you to your core, and support your choice to adopt.

Chapter Five
The Home Study

All the state-required inspections, meetings, paperwork, and training takes place during the home study. There are many boxes for the adoptive parents to check with the social worker working as the home study facilitators. Have you finished your CPR class? Check. Mental Prep Exercises? Child Birthing Lessons? Check and check.

You feel like you're back in school after all the reading assignments on diapers and comprehensive tests. Don't forget to take your fingerprints for multiple background checks and complete the 1616 form on your social and medical history and the 1693 adoption materials form. Be sure to practice for the birthing classes at your nearby hospital. You'll act like you have a leg up on birth parents because you essentially do. That is if the birth parents review and accept your medical history report. If there's ever a time when the adoption process feels like a job interview, it's during home study.

Private Adoption agencies guide adoptive parents through the home study by checking every home safety detail from kitchen fire extinguishers to door locks and staircase barricades.

Public Adoption agencies may not provide the personal prep work, but you can contact your local fire department to help prepare you for the home study inspection. Are you interested in getting an early start on home study prep? Go to American Adoptions.com for state-by-state information on adoption home studies.

Background Check

Adoptive parents with prior felonies, from DUI to resisting arrest and tax fraud, may be disqualified during the home study background checks. First and second-degree felonies will undoubtedly disqualify you for adoption. Adoptive parents with a fourth-degree or non-violent felony on their record have opportunities to defend past actions. They can persuade their home study facilitator how they've learned from their past mistakes and will make excellent parents. However, some states have strict policies regarding adoptive parents with criminal records eliminating opportunities to plead one's case.

Medical records may reveal life-threatening diseases from cancer to heart disease and HIV/AIDS. Severe illness may not "officially" disqualify you from becoming an adoptive parent, but it may essentially stop the process in its tracks.

Policies vary from state to state and between Private and Public Adoption procedures. It's valuable to be as informed as possible from the start. Check our resources like Adoption Network.com to learn of any obstacles to your adoption journey.

Training Courses

Training in Basic Life Support techniques is part of the adoption home study process. Your life support training complements parenting skills classes to prepare you for stresses like infant colic and a baby that won't sleep. Newfound skills around infant life support will prepare you for the possibilities of Sudden Infant Death Syndrome (SIDS) and complications from a low birth rate. The training courses take time, but you'll exit feeling you're up for any challenge.

References

You use reference letters for college and job applications. Prospective adopted parents need reference letters during the home study process. While job reference letters speak to your qualities as a good worker, adoption reference letters confirm your characteristics as a parent capable of providing a healthy, loving, and safe home to the adopted child. Who are good judges that speak to your parental potential? Consider family members, close friends, and church leaders. Home Study facilitators frequently require four reference letters sent directly to them.

Assessment Interviews

Chances are you've looked at sample questions in preparation for the Adoptive Family Assessment delivered by the Home Study facilitator and social worker. The Assessment Interviews, often three hours long, provides background and information regarding attitudes about parenting, childhood experiences, marital history, and your motivations to adopt. If you want to summarize the goals of the Assessment Interview, the Home Study facilitator intends to determine if you have what it takes to become a successful adoptive parent.

You may be hearing interview tips from fellow adoptive parents. Be prepared to experience different questions and formats. Our Assessment Interviewer asked us to list the characteristics we hoped to see in our adoptive child, including age and gender. Our Assessment Interview also asked us to disclose if we would consider an adopted child experiencing low birth weight, Fetal Alcohol Syndrome, or prior foster care. The Assessment Interview leaves nothing to chance regarding adoptive parents and what they will and won't accept.

Notes

Notes

Voices of Adoption:

Imagine you are applying to your dream job.
What distinguishes you from other candidates?
Concentrate on the content more
than the perfect design.

Chapter Six
Your Profile Book

Nothing captures the effort behind the adoption process like reviewing design packages for the custom Adoption Profile Books. When it comes to sharing your stories with adoption agencies and birth moms in a compelling manner, a beautifully designed Adoption Profile Book gets the job done.

An Adoption Profile Book captures a fundamental truth of the adoption process. Adoption can be a pitch competition among prospective parents looking to win the hearts and minds of birth moms. If a professionally designed Adoption Profile Book gives you and your partner an edge then the cost of putting the book together is worth every dollar.

Your adoption agency or attorney may have book specifications for you to follow. Many Adoption Profile Book templates emphasize family stories like how the prospective parents met.

Adoption Profile Book sections include tours of your home, especially a peek at the child's future room, a profile of your neighborhood, and a day-in-the-life preview of your child's future life from college savings to family pets and hiring a nanny.

Looking to capture our story professionally, my husband and I paid a designer $1500 to craft our book after reviewing examples shared by our adoption agency. We also received excellent advice from family friends practicing adoption law and started a business that designs Adoption Profile Books for prospective parents.

Nice pictures of your home and family are essential but do maintain privacy and security. I know I have a public profile as a well-known OB-GYN in Greater Cincinnati, but I would never list the address of my home in the profile book.

There are numerous online design platforms like Shutterfly and DIY templates available at more affordable costs. Some adoptive parents produce Adoption Profile videos and websites.

When selling yourself to the adoption agency and birth mother as suitable parents, you're willing to do whatever it takes within budget.

Photo Journal

Many first-time adoptive parents face an unexpected challenge when it comes to crafting their Adoption Profile Books. Birth moms and agencies want to see photos of prospective parents with young children, and, well, such images may be hard to find.

That's the case for my husband and me. Our godchildren live outside the United States, and our friends have older children. A creative project like an Adoption Profile Book forces you to be creative. Our profile book contains photos of me holding the child and of one of my patients. I can't begin to share how grateful I was that my patient agreed to come to our house, bring her beautiful baby and have a photographer take our pictures with me holding her beautiful baby dressed in our best Sunday outfits. The baby smiled and looked happy as if she understood how important this day was going to mean to us. These photos are the highlights of our book.

Who You Are

One of the things I like about the day-in-the-life portion of the Adoption Profile Book is it answers so many questions from the birth mom in a friendly and warm manner.

Will a busy professional like yourself have the time to raise a child?

Are you mostly raising the child, or will it be daycare staff, extended family, or a nanny? Do you like the look of the child's room? Do you like the picture of the child's future life?

The day-in-the-life portion of our story captures the 'support village' we've worked hard at building over the years. It also displays emotional vulnerabilities many adoptive parents share around lost children and pregnancies. Sharing this side of your story is painful, but there's a good chance the birth mom has sadness in her life, leading her to adoption.

Emotional support, that's the actual theme in the Adoption Profile Book. Beyond the size and style of your home and financial resources for education and vacations, the profile book captures the level of support from family and friends you have at your disposal when you bring your adopted child through the front door.

Parents on both sides of the adoption journey want to ensure that the child will be taken care of and loved. That's the story your Adoption Profile Book needs to share.

Openness

There are parenting books specifically about Openness in adoption for good reasons. It's likely the most crucial decision you'll make regarding the child, birth mom, and your family during the adoption journey.

Are you leaning towards an open adoption with lots of contact between you and the birth mom? Will your adoption be closed with firm boundaries around communication and plenty of distance between your family and the birth mother?

If you want to increase your chance of a birth mom choosing you over other parents, you'll want to implement Openness in your adoption.

What does Openness mean, especially regarding adoption? There will be consistent verbal and visual communication between you and the birth mom, especially for the first year or two. There's also a pledge to reassess communication after the first two years.

Sharing your stance on Openness in your Adoption Profile Book provides the birth mom with clear answers to some of her most challenging adoption questions. It communicates your values and helps build empathy.

You want a birth mom to read your Adoption Profile Book and say, 'These parents would be a good match for my child.' That's what our birth mom said to us after reading our profile book. I'm sharing these detailed tips because I want you to have that experience, too.

Notes

Voices of Adoption:

Your intuition will let you know when you have a perfect match, but be cautiously optimistic. You need to ask the hard questions to understand where the birth mother is coming from.

Chapter Seven
Finding a Match

A successful match is the fundamental goal of all adoption journeys. It's when a birth mom chooses a family, couple, or single parent to adopt her child. All the hard work in selecting an adoption agency, completing the home story, and crafting your Adoption Profile Book, results in a Successful Match. Trust me. There are no shortcuts towards landing a successful match. You have to complete all the necessary steps in the adoption journey.

Birth Mom's Profile and Prenatal Care

Prenatal care revolves around scheduled, routine visits to a doctor during pregnancy. The care ideally begins when the mother finds out they're pregnant, usually around ten weeks. The care continues with a session every four weeks for the first 28 weeks of pregnancy and increases to a session every two weeks at week 35. These prenatal best practices are essential for the delivery of a healthy baby. That's why adoptive parents need access to the birth mom's medical records and profile. There may be a history of asthma, diabetes, hypertension, smoking, or harmful drug use.

Keep digging. Go beyond the state-required medical reports and request drug screens and lab work to offset any concerns. Learn about the birth mom's family history.

There are no disrespectful questions when it comes to a baby's health. Review the medical records and ask the birth mom, "Do you smoke? Do you smoke weed? Do you use cocaine, heroin, or meth? Are there occurrences of schizophrenia or schizoaffective disorder in your family?

Is there a history of mood disorders, behavioral disorders, ADHD, depression, anxiety, or psychosis? Are there any genetic disorders or inheritable diseases like hemophilia or cystic fibrosis?

You're asking for the baby's health because the birth mom's answers will determine any immediate care before any tests.

The medical history of my daughter, our daughter's birth mom, is far less traumatic. There's a history of eczema, and, sure enough, our daughter also suffers from eczema.

Step aside from the medical records briefly and ask the birth mom about her home life and how she became an expectant mother. Learn about her childhood and the birth father. Show her that you care and you're not making judgments. Lead a discussion about her extended family, including mom, dad, sister, brother, grandparents, on her side and the birth father's side. Your goal is to attain the most comprehensive medical history possible. You'll learn her whole story about coming to adoption and share your tale.

I remember having a woman-to-woman conversation with our daughter's birth mom and learning she didn't want to keep her baby but lacked the resources to end her pregnancy safely.

Adoption agency staff members are frequently onsite with the birth mom at her doctor's visits. They can provide the medical information you need to determine your interest in "matching."

What you learn may bring comfort or worry. The birth mom's medical history may fall within or outside your tolerance guidelines for continuing with the adoption.

Would you be okay with a birth mom with a history of heroin use? That's a dealbreaker for me. Are you alright with the occasional use of weed? What's more impactful, alcohol use, drug history, or psychiatric concerns?

There's no such thing as too much medical information when deciding on an adoption match. Either way, this is valuable information to have and more extensive than any agency profile. You'll use it immediately and continue to access it as your adopted child grows older.

Birth Mom Interview

You may think that making arrangements for the birth mom interview are low-key and easy, but you would be wrong. The birth mom interview is an essential part of the adoption journey and warrants extra attention.

First, choose a convenient and neutral space like the adoption agency offices or a restaurant. Allowing the adoption agency to host or set up the meeting would be a good idea. If you're responsible for managing the birth mom interview, be sure to respect the birth mom's time and work schedules. The meeting space needs to feel comfortable, familiar, and private enough for meaningful conversations. In case you're wondering, draw a red line through your home or workspace. You do not want the birth mom to feel subpar because she's on your turf.

Many steps throughout the adoption process are nerve-wracking. Meeting birth moms for the first time can make you anxious, but mostly, the experience is exciting. You're getting to know a key person who, sight unseen, is considering helping you grow your family. Now that's someone you have to meet. Plus, they want to learn your story, too.

Instead of sweating something that feels like the most impactful meeting of your life, remember to remain forthcoming, honest, and transparent about your emotions and hopes for parenthood. Keep the conversation casual and fluid. You don't want to do all the talking like a salesman making a desperate pitch. Let your spouse or partner play an active role in the conversation. I remember nudging my husband repeatedly and asking him to answer questions. Allow the birth mom to lead the interview. If you're honest, it's impossible to be false or answer questions incorrectly.

Your adoption agency will likely share prep questions. During our interview, the birth mom, my husband, and I talked about education, our commitment to public schools, respect for teachers, readiness to begin saving for the child's college, and our pledge to play an active role in our child's education. My husband is a former teacher, so you can imagine our conversation was heartfelt and passionate.

The birth mom asked about family pets and whether we preferred a girl or a boy. She wanted to know our adoption journey, our love for children, and how we decided to adopt. As I said, there was transparency on both sides of the table.

Be prepared to share your personal story. The birth mom wanted to know about our families. I talked about growing up in an inspiring, female-led environment and how my mom raised me as her mom raised her.

The three of us talked about community, gratitude, partnerships, relationships. We talked about giving back to communities and helping others and how we planned to inspire that value in our adopted child.

I shared how I'm the product of four generations of strong women, and I believed my story emotionally moved her.

I believe that adoption agencies call this a "birth mom interview" for many reasons. One, they want prospective parents to take it seriously, and for me, that means dressing appropriately.

Think a lot about who you're sitting across during the interview.

What do you want your clothes to say about you? Remember, you don't want the birth mom to feel subpar. I'm an OB-GYN and proud of my work, but I would never wear scrubs or a lab coat to the interview to emphasize my career status.

My goal was to look polished and presentable, and, yes, that included good lipstick. I wanted the birth mom to feel she's talking with two professional people who will deliver a clean, healthy, organized, two-parent life to her child. I also shared that we planned to adopt one time, and her baby would receive the attention of a single child.

Do you know the phrase 'you can't judge a book by its cover?' Well, I say, why take a chance? Make a beautiful cover.

Notes

Notes

Voices of Adoption:

The baby's ours! — Or is she?

Chapter Eight
Bringing the Baby Home

I attended two neonatal appointments with the birth mom before she made a match. I mostly listened, learned, and observed, never revealing my work as an OB-GYN.

I fully expected the neonatal physician to be cooperative and answer the questions of a prospective adoptive parent coming to the appointment. Looking back, I realize that I was expecting too much.

I wanted to speak to the doctor about the birth mom's ultrasound. The doctor disagreed. While I did not reveal myself as an experienced OB-GYN, I could not stop acting like an OB-GYN. I looked at the birth's mom's ultrasound pictures and report, listened to the inaccurate interpretation by the ultrasound technician, and tried to interject for the birth mom's benefit.

Remember, the birth mom hadn't made her final decision, and the baby was not officially ours yet. Still, as an OB-GYN, my commitment to the well-being of pregnant women is 24/7. I wasn't going to leave the appointment without getting answers about the birth mom's negative blood type and heightened chance for a fetal anemia.

You have to be ready for anything throughout the adoption journey. I know that my experience at the birth mom's prenatal visit was unique. My role as an OB-GYN capable of seeing red flags for potential delivery issues makes my situation even more one-of-a-kind. You can still learn from it.

I soon revealed my identity as an OB-GYN because of my growing worry around the birth mom's health.

I grew concerned about a potential anemia for the baby and the need to test the birth mom's antibodies. Would the birth mom's doctor respond in time? Would the mom receive an injection of Rhogam, an anti-D immune globulin for pregnant women, the moment she needs it? As an OB-GYN, my mind raced towards the risks of anemia in the baby.

At a phase in the adoption journey when prospective parents should grow excited, I became more and more aggravated and demanded transparency from the birth mom's doctors. I'm concerned about the health of the birth mom and the baby, likely, my future child. I can't stop being an advocate for women's health.

It's just a couple of days before Christmas, holiday stress is in full throttle, and I decided as a prospective parent and OB-GYN that I would do everything possible to ensure the birth mom would receive the best care. I didn't care how I would come across.

I shared pointed advice about antenatal testing and steroids to help with the baby's lung development. I questioned management decisions around the birth mom's care. Was her doctor shuffling through too many patients? Was the birth mom being treated differently as a Medicaid patient? I came close to reporting the doctor on the spot until my husband persuaded me to wait.

I'm sharing this very personal chapter from my adoption journey because there are universal lessons for all adoptive parents.

There are times when your commitment to the adoption and advocacy for the child will rise and appear aggressive. People may think you are a bully with a bad temper. That's what the birth mom told our adoption agency. She wondered if I would lose my temper with an adoptive child the way I argued with her doctors. I told her I was sorry that I frightened her, but as an OB-GYN, I never back down when it comes to a woman's health and the health of her unborn child. I shared the same sentiment with the adoption agency.

If I scared the birth mom away and she chose a different family because of my behavior, fine, I can live with that decision.

Behind the scenes, I remained every bit the birth mom's advocate, demanding she receive complete documentation of her medical conditions. I persuaded the birth mom that my fight for her excellent medical care showed how I'd fight for the baby.

Per the adoption agency's advice, my husband became the face of the adoptive family when dealing with the birth mom and her doctors.

Preparing for your Bundle's Arrival

Are you reviewing the facts from your training classes? When the baby arrives, you'll have no time for deliberation. Adoptive parents need to act fast.

The books *What to Expect When You're Expecting* and *What to Expect In The First Year of Life* are popular for good reasons. Buy and read them. They'll prevent unnecessary phone calls to your doctor.

Preparing yourself to make a fast adoption decision is in your control. What about adoption factors that aren't in your control? Be ready to react to the many external factors inherent to an adoption decision.

What if the birth mom wants a closed adoption and you're limited to the existing medical history and information. You'll have to say, 'nay, or yay,' based on the info at hand. Are you ready? What if it's a public adoption, and you learn that the birth mom has a long-ago history of heroin use? Are you still prepared?

If you have planned for what's in your control and out of your control, I believe you will be ready when your bundle arrives.

The BIRTH Day

All your adoption prep and planning brings you to the BIRTH day, the moment when your adopted baby arrives. You won't want to miss one moment.

Closer to the delivery date, my husband and I drove to a hotel near where the birth mom lives. We did not want to leave anything to chance.

An adoption BIRTH day is a communal event. You're playing an integral role, so plan accordingly.

Arrive at the hospital, birthing center, or home with a baby bag filled with clothes. Bring every possible item the baby may need, like blankets, shoes, diapers, and formula. Do not plan for any supplies from the hospital. Your responsibilities as a parent begin now.

Review information from your pediatrician sessions. All parents, especially adoptive parents, have to think on their feet.

The more you prepare, the more joyous the first of many BIRTH days will turn out to be.

Surrender Day

The concept of an adopted child's BIRTH day is clear to everyone, even when you spell it in all caps.

However, Surrender Day, a significant event in the adoption process, requires some explanation. Sometime between 24 and 72 hours (depending on the state), a birth mom permanently surrenders parental rights to the adoptive parents. Think of BIRTH day as the emotional and real-life adoption of the baby and Surrender Day as the follow-up, legal confirmation. It's also time when the birth mom can reflect and treat her post-adoption depression before signing the final paperwork.

Just as there are closed and open adoption processes, there are also rare cases regarding coercion and fraud where the birth mom revokes her original consent agreement.

Chances are you'll experience similar circumstances like our process with our daughter. Adoption Agency staff will inform you when you can see the newly born baby. They'll schedule a meeting, likely at the hospital, where you and the birth mother can sign the surrender form. Some states require the birth mom to wait a few days to get through her post-adoption emotions. When that occurs, adoption staff will complete the surrender paperwork with the birth mom and schedule the baby's hospital discharge to the adoptive parents.

With the paperwork signed and delivered, Adoption Agency Assessors will visit the home over multiple months to observe you, the house, the baby, and complete home study assessments. During the post-surrender period, you'll share growth charts, proof of vaccinations, and updated medical charts.

By the third home study visit, you'll likely experience adoption paperwork and supervision fatigue. It's okay. We all feel it, but the fact that your baby is home in your arms makes it worthwhile.

Putative Father Registry

Here we are describing the adopted baby in its new home and adoptive mother's arms, and we've yet to discuss the birth father in any detail.

The fact is that many adoptions revolve around the birth mom and the adoptive parents, with the birth father frequently absent and unknown.

States grant unwed birth fathers various opportunities to claim rights and establish paternity through father registries like the Putative Father Registry. Birth fathers that register 30 days or sooner after the baby's birth receive notice of the baby's adoption and a chance to object to the adoption.

The possibility of a birth father contesting an adoption after the baby's birth and late in the adoption process likely makes you feel like there's no end to the challenges facing adoptive parents. Once again, adoptive parents have to prepare for anything with the help of their adoption attorney and agency.

Find comfort in the guidance of professional organizations like the Academy of Adoption and Assisted Reproduction Attorneys and state laws protecting the interests of the children and adoptive families.

Birth fathers have to meet eligibility requirements and register their paternity through state-approved, hospital-approved programs. These policies protect all parties, including the child.

Notes

Voices of Adoption:

Be flexible and malleable. Your life has radically changed — you are a parent now. Give yourself time to adjust.

Chapter Nine
The Final Hurdle

A deep exhale of relief may be the sign that you passed the Final Hurdle and your adoption is complete.

You may be expressing a feeling of joy like never before and sharing endless smartphone snaps with family members and friends.

I remember sitting with our daughter on the drive back from the hospital. I'm in the car's backseat doing the tasks that newborn parents do. I'm changing diapers and reaching for the formula bottle. These actions will soon become mundane, but now, they feel miraculous.

"Oh my gosh, okay, so this is real," I said aloud. "We're officially parents, and we'll need to figure this out."

I'm an experienced OB-GYN, yet, I would closely watch our daughter breathing to ensure everything was fine. Each whimper made me nervous. I obsessed over the growing number of her wet diapers. I seriously considered that my baby was developing a urinary tract infection. It's funny how years of medical training fail to stop you from becoming a nervous mom.

My adoption journey is one-of-a-kind. It started that way, and of course, it will wrap that way.

Two weeks after bringing our daughter home, I underwent cancer surgery just when I wanted to rest and spend solo time with my baby.

Life throws punches, and adoptive parents know that better than anyone. You adjust to the challenges. You keep moving and focus on one obstacle at a time, from a delay in the adoption process to a diagnosis of cancer.

Sometimes, life gives you breaks. My cancer didn't include chemo, so I returned to mama duties faster than planned.

My husband took charge of baby duties during surgery and recovery. We pushed the baby's 'Sip and See' party for family and friends three months down the road, along with a church blessing ceremony.

I remember being tired from the surgery, but the love and spirit from faraway family and friends who traveled great distances to celebrate the baby ignited me like the best medicine.

"Girl, this looks like a wedding reception," my best friends told me, picking up individually wrapped cookies and gift bags with my daughter's personalized bottles of hand sanitizer. "Regina's finally a momma!" Why hand sanitizer? A new baby requires extra precautions, but there's no stopping the joy and celebration amongst friends and family praising an adopted baby. I had friends and family travel from across the country to witness this miracle. Their presence and support will never be forgotten.

Establishing a Routine

Our first months with our daughter were anything but routine. I'm recovering from cancer surgery and am extra worried about her newborn immune system. Family visits outside my mom and stepdad would have to wait.

My mom and husband joined in taking care of the baby and me, trading baby shifts to sleep and drive me to doctor's appointments. We figured out schedules on the fly. Looking back, it was a magical time of close togetherness.

My cancer recovery led to a quieter routine for my family and me, but I recommend creating a private space for the new mama and baby. You'll want to adjust, heal, and connect. Privacy helps when crafting sleep routines and responding to her cries.

I enjoyed sharing my new experiences as a mama with our adoption agency social worker during follow-up appointments. It felt like I had two support systems. There's my family at home and the adoption staff member outside my house.

Work-Life Balance

Women are becoming mothers later in life, but I tilt the median age more than anyone. I'm writing this book at 48 after becoming a first-time mom at 47.

My sorority sisters, many of them with college-age kids, tell me, "Whitfield, we don't envy you at all. We are over child-care issues." I understand their positions, but I still chuckle when they tease me. I love being a later-in-life mom.

I'm receiving great advice from family and friends, even my sorority girls, but the best tips come from doing the work and spending time with your baby and spouse.

Everyone describes the adoption process as a journey because it's true. It's also a whirlwind of twists and turns. Trust me. You'll want a trusted partner to help you navigate.

I laugh a lot thinking about what would be different if I became a mama at 28 instead of 48. I'm like, "Well, I definitely would have more energy. I would also be less patient."

At 48, deep in a medical career, I also clearly understand why moms want to spend more time at home and think creatively to make the home time happen. You don't want to miss a thing from new phrases learned at daycare to playtime at home.

Treating parenting like a science project, I have a Venn diagram on a wall at home helping my husband and me see our shared baby duties and responsibilities.

At our home, there's none of this storming off and saying, "Oh well, I was planning on doing this today." The adoption process requires organization, but there are moments when you have to act fast and think by the 'seat of your pants.'

My husband and I talk to each other. "What is your schedule looking like today? And are you going to be able to pick her up? I don't get off until later. Can you get her?"

There's no Work-Life Balance with two working parents in separate silos. You'll need communication, organization, shared responsibilities, and some of that think-on-your-feet strategizing you learned during the adoption process. That's extra true if your partner travels for work.

Now, establishing Work-Life Balance means the woman has the opportunity to resume her work thoroughly. If a busy OB-GYN can restart her career while maintaining Work-Life Balance, I think just about any mom can do it if given a chance.

The catch is that I eased back to work, starting at two weeks of a partial schedule, then returning to an adjusted, 8 am to 4 pm workday free of early morning and late-in-day appointments, including C-sections and other surgeries. I want to make sure I'm available on days when my husband isn't.

Great organization and communication is the best way for achieving Work-Life Balance. Working mamas can achieve it and enjoy both worlds. It's an example that hopefully inspires mamas to return to their careers and work if that's what they want to do.

Adoption Finalization Day

People outside the adoption community think adoptions are official when adoptive parents bring the baby home. Adoptive parents know differently. The finalization of an adoption, or the Finalization Day, occurs after the home study assessments, past the time when a birth father can claim rights and establish paternity, and after the time when a birth mother can revoke her adoption consent agreement.

Additional legal documents and court procedures for adoptive parents to complete, including a decree of adoption to confirm any remaining details like hospital bills and paying living expenses to the birth mother.

It's a long, emotional journey to Finalization Day, but I don't know any adoptive parents who regret the hard work.

Our Finalization Day took place in a courtroom to complete our daughter's decree of adoption paperwork. We never once complained about the long 167 mile drive one way to address any of her or the birth mom's concerns. Our judge made the courtroom process feel more like a celebration. We took group photos and received a gift of a replica judge's gavel for our daughter.

The adoption agency was there with more gifts for our daughter. I kept repeating, "Oh my gosh. It is over. She's finally ours!"

There were additional court papers to file, but Finalization Day felt like crossing the adoption finish line. Our daughter was born in January of 2018. Our Finalization Day took place in September of the same year and approximately two years after we made the decision to adopt. Was it hard? Absolutely, but I cannot imagine a better way to spend two years.

To get your questions answered about life after adoption, take part in conversations with other adoptive parents. Gather all the credible and useful information you can. Give yourself momma breaks and schedule date nights with your partner and friends.

Learn to trust members of your support village with caring for your baby. Remember you cannot be available 24 hours a day for everybody. Accept the help that is offered to you.

Don't sweat the small stuff, or you will become aggravated all the time. There will be adjustments. I have to admit that I'm a neat freak — someone who lines their shoes at the door when entering the home and sweeping the moment a crumb hits the kitchen floor. When our daughter picks up her bowl of cereal, eats some, then pours the rest on the floor, I have to fight the urge to vacuum immediately. My hubby says, "Regina, she's a child. She's going to do that."

My hubby and I are fussing over spilled cereal, and our daughter listens and says, "Mom, Mom, I don't want to hear you fussing. You and daddy can't talk like that." I'm thinking, "Oh my goodness, she's picking this up at three?"

You have to adjust and find balance. You have to choose your battles.

I'm not fussy with my hair. I'm pulling it back into a ponytail woman. After listening to my mom fuss about our daughter's hair, I scheduled the time to be away from work and take my baby to get her hair done. That's a lot of effort and time, but our daughter's hair looked pretty. That is, until at home, while I'm sleeping from exhaustion, and our daughter dumps an entire container of grease and oil onto her braids. I wanted to scream, I was so upset; until my mom reminded me.

"You did the same thing when you were a baby," my mom said, laughing. "That's what three-year-olds do. Just be glad she didn't have the scissors and decide to give you a haircut in the process during your nap."

There will be stressful moments and times when you question your qualities as a parent. Don't be hard on yourself. There will be situations that you don't know how to handle. Return to your think-on-your-feet experience and figure out what's best for you, your baby, and your partner.

If you don't, you'll become consistently totally exhausted and partially resentful.

There are many ways to accomplish Work-Life Balance. You may wish there was a single road map for raising a baby right. There isn't. Craft a road map that works best for your family. Just don't let opportunities fade away.

Notes

Notes

Voices of Adoption:

While you grow into your new parenting role, think ahead to the next steps for your child's future in your life.

Chapter Ten
Your Life After Adoption

Since becoming a mom, one of many changes I value is hearing people tell me, "I like how you don't sweat the small stuff."

That's a new thing for me. As an OB-GYN, my work requires me to pay attention to little details that may grow into significant medical issues.

Becoming a mom and raising a child reminds you that you're not in charge of everything. If you become aggravated every time your baby spills cereal on the floor, you'll be angry all of the time.

I have a new mama rule to share. If something is not going to cause undue harm to your child, it may have to wait until tomorrow. Our daughter helps with that rule by yelling out after she has fallen off the chair to the floor; "I'm okay."

If your baby covers her face in colored markers or draws flowers on the bedroom wall, grab a washcloth, remind her that we have paper for drawing flowers and deal with it gracefully.

When our daughter draws on the back of my laptop instead of the paper I handed to her, I exhale, grab some cleaning wipes, and refuse to let it bother me. On extra calm days, I even attempt to turn the situation into a teachable moment by giving her the wipes to clean the mess she's made.

Just deciding how to best talk to your child requires patience. Do you speak like an adult? Are there appropriate times for "talking like a baby?"

Our daughter points at me and asks, "What is that," and I answer her in an adult manner, "That is a breast." She becomes excited and says, "Oh, I have breasts!" Later, at the dinner table, we're eating chicken breasts, and she says, "Oh my gosh, you're eating the chicken's breast? Can we eat your breast mommy?"

Type A people who thrive on organization and structure learn to be more carefree and Type B-like when it comes to the basket of laundry sitting on the sofa. Tell yourself; it will get done eventually, but right now, I'm focusing on important things like time with my child, eating, and sleeping.

I'm 51 years young. I'm 13 years young in my second career as an OB-GYN, and I have no plans to become a stay-at-home mom. My after-adoption career changes involve adjusting my work schedule.

I enjoy what I do, and I enjoy raising my child, and I'm figuring out how to balance it all. I admit to feeling rushed too many times and saying to myself, "The weather is beautiful. It would be nice to sit out on the deck and take in the warmth instead of being in the office working."

I think back to what my mom tells me repeatedly. You work hard and sacrifice on the front end to enjoy the fruits of your labor on the back end of life. Seize the energy and strength you have now to work smarter and not harder. You will build today what you can enjoy tomorrow. Your baby may ask for you constantly today, but she'll be fine after reaching for a book or toy. She won't remember at the age of three (3) how many days you were not at home or the days you were on a 24 hour call. She will remember at age 13 whether you were present for her activities. She will grow to appreciate your work ethic.

Changes

I tell my family and friends that becoming a mama changes some things but not everything. What changes? I would say expectations, goals, perspective, and your long-term and short-term plans.

What stays the same? Becoming a mama doesn't change who you are at your core, and still, I do think about all the changes for me.

I am no longer taking time for granted. I've experienced first-hand how fast our daughter is growing after looking at pictures of her from just a few years ago.

My priorities are different. I'm working extra hard now, so I'll have extra time with our daughter in the next few years. I remember making my health a priority when pregnant, but I'm aggressively making fitness a priority today. It's surprising how much energy I have for my career and home despite working approximately 60 hours per week.

My adoption journey makes me different from friends like my sorority girls because I did not become a mama in my 20s. I've come to value the difference and the playful dynamic it creates with my friends.

My friends and I are planning our 35th anniversary in the sorority in 2024, and we're saying, "Maybe we can have an event where we bring our children, and they can meet each other? Our kids can babysit your daughter for you so you can let your hair down." Isn't that wonderful? My sorority girls and I are different when it comes to being mamas, but that difference makes for some magical times.

I'm typically a vocal person who immediately shares what I feel and want. Let me refresh that as a mama. I no longer vocalize my in-the-moment frustrations. While I aim to collaborate on schedules and workloads with my coworkers, I cannot control everything work-wise.

It's funny to hear me admit this, but I accept that I'm a number in a large medical enterprise competing with other practices for customers. I think about business systems and the priority of attracting patients. I don't believe I felt that way coming out of residency.

I'm more patient than I used to be, and I credit our daughter for that growth and maturity. I no longer allow long workdays to upset me because I know I'm doing it for our daughter's wellbeing. I want to spend more time at home in the next few years. I want to build generational wealth for our family. I still love being a doctor, but I love coming home to my baby and being a mama and a wife.

I began my adoption journey convinced that becoming a mama would change who I am, and now, I'm convinced that being a parent has changed my perspective on just about everything. I'm aware of a few people stuck in their previous mindset despite getting married and having kids. That's not me; and, that's not many of the mamas and papas that I know who cared when they became parents — no matter what the age they are in their lives at the time. Like me, they just want to be open to loving someone who needs it.

Nurturing New Relationships
While Maintaining Old Relationships

Babies absorb lots of time and can wrap up your life. Be proactive and make time for extended family and friends. They'll want to visit with the baby, and you'll value the opportunities to stay connected. Staying close to friends even when mama duties feel overwhelming is always essential.

Maintaining my good friendships was top of mind when reading about a women-after-50 health conference in the Grand Cayman Conference. I knew it was a perfect career development and educational experience. I also saw it as an affordable girl's getaway weekend after my husband passed due to his work schedule.

I grew more excited about the Grand Cayman Islands trip after thinking about my wedding party 13 years ago. We kept in touch by phone but I had not seen some of my girls since that time.

These are friends with kids; though none with toddlers, others have grown and are in the military. One friend is six-weeks older than me because our mamas were friends and pregnant at the same time. She has been my friend literally for 51 years. Another friend in New Orleans became a competitive marathoner after losing a 20-year-old son to violent crime and after her daughter graduated from college. One of my most memorable trips was when my mom and I joined her on a running trip in Cuba.

When planning this trip, I called them all and invited them to join me. What did I hear? "Girl, I'm already there," one friend told me. "You send me your itinerary."

I'm a busy physician and new mom working hard at building Work-Life Balance but planning my Grand Cayman Islands trip with longtime girlfriends confirmed the importance of maintaining friendships.

These friends helped me through the years with prayers, donations, gifts, and simply being there when I needed support. I wouldn't be an OB-GYN without them. I wouldn't be a mama without them.

Friends can keep you grounded when you need it. They pull you out of career silos and remind you of the importance of community and interacting with others.

Friends are your support village. If you won't sustain friendships with a trip to the Grand Cayman Islands or a casual lunch at your home, what will you maintain?

Updating Important Documents

The adoption paperwork list doesn't end at Finalization Day and after bringing your child home. There likely will be a name change and a refresh of the original birth certificate, passport, and Social Security card. You'll need to visit federal offices like the Social Security Administration. You'll also want to review your child's paperwork annually and update medical coverage and documents. If you think getting a passport is time-consuming, wait for car insurance.

Chances are you have a family will. If you don't, crafting a will and trust will become a priority. Our initial estate planning includes our god-children as beneficiaries and my mother as guardian and power of attorney. The updated will and trust list our daughter as the primary beneficiary and spell out guardian details if my husband and I pass simultaneously.

The paperwork feels overwhelming to me because it's constant. There are always offices to call, forms to sign, information to gather, and tax documents to check. Luckily, adoption makes parents experts at bureaucracy. So you got this!

Adjusting Budget

In my household, we establish short and long-term goals. Every six months, we look at current bills and identify where we can shave expenses. Raising our daughter changes the budget formula. There are 529 savings plans for college and a Gerber Life Insurance policy.

Adopting a baby certainly adds expenses, but I remain committed to zero consumer debt and small monthly budgets of $500 or less for leisure expenses. If you want to spend more money, be prepared to adjust your retirement goals.

I take the same short and long-term approach when crafting a budget for our daughter. I also have key questions that I ask myself when thinking about savings. Am I willing to give up item A, high-quality childcare, for example, to buy item B?

Remember the support village we've been talking about throughout the book? Adjusting budgets requires some critical additions to the support village. Hire a financial advisor skilled at family estate planning and an accountant. They'll quickly become the members of the support village that you talk to most often.

Establishing a Village of Support

Forget about adoption paperwork. Establishing and growing your support village will be an ongoing commitment and require hard work. It's hard because there are few things as important as gathering support.

I come from a small family, so there aren't many cousins for baby watching and frequent playdates.

Even the best work-life balance fails to provide extra time at school to befriend fellow parents and establish new friends. Sometimes I feel like we're always running. That's when I pause and work on my support village.

I post on Facebook groups for physician moms. I post updates when I'm heading to the hospital if moms in my group will also be there.

When moms in our social group share experiences on nannies, I post feedback. I want them to feel like they're part of my support village.

Notes

Notes

> *Voices of Adoption:*
>
> **It is very helpful to have a village surrounding you with love and support as you raise your child. No man is an island.**

Conclusion

Are you feeling more prepared for the adoption process? If you're on the fence, are you now more likely to choose adoption? I hope this book convinces you to join the community of adopted parents.

My dreams of becoming a mama were realized, thanks to adoption. I know it will help you realize your dreams as well, no matter where you are in life.

Think about me, a later-in-life mom. Know that it's never too late to make family dreams come true. This book is part of that dream for me. I have chosen to share my unique adoption journey and story to inspire mature women that becoming a mama is not out of reach despite what the naysayers say. Also, I want to touch the hearts of all potential BIRTH moms who are considering her options. To save a life and give that life to another not only brings joy to the child but also to the adoptive parents.

I've pulled back the curtain on many of my heartbreaks and disappointments involving my fertility and medical challenges so you can see that ALL things are possible, and what God has for you IS for you if you only believe. If my adoption story gives women courage and hope, my risk of telling my story is well worth it.

People frequently ask me how I manage. Some focus on the long work hours of an OB-GYN. Others are speaking of my breast cancer, miscarriages, and struggle to become pregnant. I'm here to share with you that people will ask you the same questions. All parents hear that question because there's always so much to handle with too little time. Yet, we get it done!

My husband, a rare parent who gets eight hours of sleep every night, continues to inspire me. Despite the craziness of both of our work schedules, he maintains the balance and voice of reason in our home, our discussion, and the direction for our family. Never has there been a time since bringing our daughter home that he has not been there to address her every need — from diaper changing to baths to combing her hair. He is ever present for the both of us, and I am eternally grateful.

Our Daughter

My daughter is caring. I'm not taking credit for teaching it to her. It's how she is. When I'm sleepy or not feeling well, our daughter will say, "Oh, Mommy, are you okay?" And when I had my foot surgery, our daughter wanted to kiss my foot to make it better.

A caring child makes you more loving. My husband and I learned to talk to our daughter instead of yelling. We persuade instead of scolding her.

My mom tells me, "Don't negotiate with a child — she is three." My mom also says, "Sure she can make the decision whether she will wear the blue or purple dress to school today, but not about whether or not she will take the medicine to combat the fever that she has." One of my daughter's favorite sayings now is "I don't want to". But I explain, we're not negotiating. We're communicating, and we've become better communicators because of our daughter.

Everyone has a role to play in adoption, and you have to perform respectfully. You and your support tribe have responsibilities, and you have a greater chance for success when you act as a team.

Performing your roles means recognizing the value of life and appreciating each day to the fullest. Being a productive member of your support tribe demands focus, hard work, and perseverance.

I remember my mom repeatedly saying, "'Impossible, never, and cannot' are words that should not be part of your vocabulary. If you use these words, you limit yourself." It's a mindset. She supported our decision to adopt and she loved me through my pain — a pain she had experienced years before.

As experiences come full circle, I would like to thank you, the reader, for inspiring me to revisit my challenges, face my disappointments, and celebrate my wins of becoming a loving wife, mother, and author. Thank you for sharing this body of work.

Resources

Further Reading
- Healthline, "The Best Adoption Blogs of 2020" www.healthline.com/health/parenting/best-adoption-blogs#1
- Adoption Circle, "Book Resources: Books for Children, Teens, and Adults" www.adoptioncircle.org/adoption-resources/book-resources/

Adoption Resources
- Adoption.org
- EmbryoAdoption.org
- InThisWithYou.org
- FreeAdoptionHelp.com
- ThreeStrandsInc.org
- BraveLove.org
- OYFF.org
- Ohio Department of Job and Family Services, "Child Characteristics Checklist for Foster Care and/or Adoption" homestudyohio.com/static/media/Child_Characteristics_Checklist_ODJFS_Form_2013.22f6df8c.pdf

Financial Resources
- Annie E. Casey Foundation, "Adoption Resources" www.aecf.org/topics/adoption
- North American Council on Adoptable Children, "US Adoption Assistance/Subsidy" www.nacac.org/help/adoption-assistance/adoption-assistance-us/
- Child Welfare Information Gateway, "Adoption & Guardian Assistance by State" www.childwelfare.gov/topics/adoption/adopt-assistance/
- Benefits.gov
- Golden Dawn Adoption Assistance Inc. www.goldendawnaa.org/

www.ingramcontent.com/pod-product-compliance
Lightning Source LLC
Chambersburg PA
CBHW051607170426
43196CB00038B/2953